new L𝑉

4ᵪ 4/6a - 9/09
5ᵪ (3/10) 4/2/13

3 ⅹ 3/05 9/05

Biographies

Ferdinand MAGELLAN

by Mervyn D. Kaufman

Consultant:

John P. Boubel, Ph.D.
History Professor, Bethany Lutheran College
Mankato, Minnesota

Capstone
press

Mankato, Minnesota

Fact Finders is published by Capstone Press
151 Good Counsel Drive, P.O. Box 669, Mankato, Minnesota 56002
www.capstonepress.com

Library of Congress Cataloging-in-Publication Data
Kaufman, Mervyn D.
    Ferdinand Magellan / by Mervyn D. Kaufman.
    p. cm.—(Fact finders. Biographies)
    Summary: An introduction to the life of sixteenth-century Portuguese explorer
Ferdinand Magellan, who found a passage for ships to sail west from the Atlantic to the
Pacific Ocean.
    Includes bibliographical references and index.
    ISBN 0-7368-2487-1 (hardcover)
    1. Magalhães, Fernão de, d. 1521—Travel—Juvenile literature. 2. Explorers—Portugal—
Biography—Juvenile literature. 3. Voyages around the world—Juvenile literature.
[1. Magellan, Ferdinand, d. 1521. 2. Explorers. 3. Voyages around the world.]
I. Title. II. Series.
G286.M2K38 2004
910'.92—dc22   2003015255

Editorial Credits
Roberta Schmidt, editor; Juliette Peters, designer; Linda Clavel and Heather
    Kindseth, illustrators; Deirdre Barton and Kelly Garvin, photo researchers;
    Eric Kudalis, product planning editor

Photo Credits
Art Resource/Chateaux de Versailles et Trianon, cover; Giraudon, 10
Bridgeman Art Library/The Stapleton Collection/Private Collection, 17
Corbis, 8–9; George W. Wright, 6–7
Corel, 18
Getty Images/Hulton Archive, 1, 4–5, 12, 13
Mary Evans Picture Library, 16, 22
North Wind Picture Archives, 11, 14–15, 19, 23, 24–25
Stock Montage Inc., 21

1 2 3 4 5 6 09 08 07 06 05 04

Table of Contents

Chapter 1 The Passage 4

Chapter 2 A Portuguese Beginning 6

Chapter 3 The Urge to Explore 8

Chapter 4 The Voyage 14

Chapter 5 Victory 20

Chapter 6 Completing the Circle 24

Map: The Voyage around the World, 1519–1522 27

Fast Facts 28

Time Line 29

Glossary 30

Internet Sites 31

Read More 31

Index 32

The Passage

On October 21, 1520, Captain General Ferdinand Magellan was waiting. He had sent two of his five ships into a **bay**. No one had seen the two ships for two days.

Magellan was looking for a way to the other side of the Americas. He believed there was a water passage, or **strait**, through the land. Magellan and his ships had been searching the coast of South America for 10 months. They had not found a strait.

Suddenly, cannons boomed in the distance. The two ships were sailing back. They were flying all of their flags.

Magellan found a waterway from the Atlantic Ocean to the Pacific Ocean.

Magellan knew what the cannons and flags meant. He had been right. There was a strait. They had found it. Later, the strait was named the Strait of Magellan.

Chapter 2

A Portuguese Beginning

Ferdinand Magellan was born in 1480 in Portugal. Ferdinand Magellan was his English name. In Portuguese, his name was Fernão de Magalhães. His parents were Rui de Magalhães and Alda de Mesquita.

At age 12, Magellan became a **page** for the queen of Portugal. He studied music, dance, hunting, and fighting. He also learned about stars.

Magellan left Portugal when he was 25 years old. He joined men sailing to India. They hoped to find new lands to **claim** for Portugal.

Magellan may have been born in Porto, Portugal. Today, the town looks different from how it was in the 1400s.

Over the next eight years, Magellan visited many places in Africa, India, and Asia. He also fought in many battles. He became known as a strong and brave leader.

Chapter 3

The Urge to Explore

Magellan grew up during the Age of Exploration. Between 1400 and 1600, many Europeans **explored** unknown areas. They learned about countries outside of Europe. Magellan was 12 years old when Christopher Columbus crossed the Atlantic Ocean. He was 18 when Vasco da Gama went around the southern tip of Africa and sailed to India. Magellan wanted to be like Columbus and da Gama. He wanted to be an explorer.

This 1590s map of the Americas shows pictures of Christopher Columbus (upper left), Amerigo Vespucci (upper right), Magellan (lower left), and Francisco Pizarro (lower right). ➤

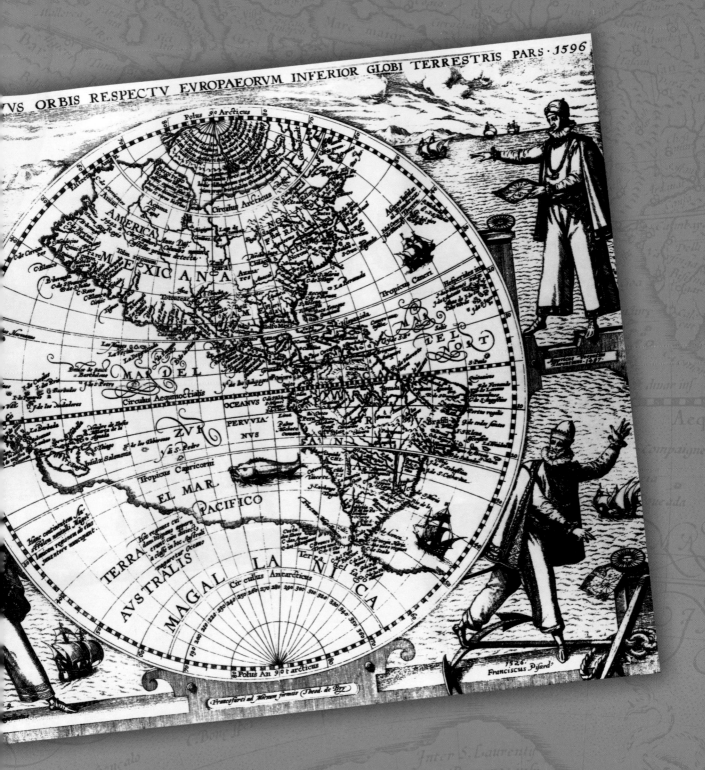

▲ Many spices came from islands in southeastern Asia. Europeans called them the Spice Islands. Today, the islands are called the Moluccas.

Explorers had many reasons for sailing into unknown areas. Some people wanted to find new lands. Some wanted to teach other people about their religion. Many explorers were looking for better trade routes between Europe and Asia.

Far East Trade

In the 1400s, goods from Asia and India were very valuable in Europe. Asia and India had silk and spices not found in Europe. The Europeans wanted the spices to make their food taste better. They wanted the silk for their clothing.

▲ For hundreds of years, most trade with Asia was done overland with camels.

Trade during the 1400s was difficult. Asia and India were far away from Europe. It took years to get goods back and forth. European traders also had to pay people who controlled the trade routes. Many European countries, such as Portugal and Spain, were looking for ways to control the trade themselves.

King Manuel of Portugal did not want to help Magellan.

Magellan's First Plan

Magellan wanted to lead Portuguese trade ships to the Spice Islands in southeastern Asia. To get there, he planned to sail around the tip of Africa and then head out to sea. He hoped to find new lands to claim for Portugal.

In 1516, Magellan went to the king of Portugal. Magellan asked King Manuel for men, ships, and supplies. King Manuel was not interested in Magellan's plan. He said no.

A New Plan

Two years later, Magellan went to Spain. He told King Charles about a new plan to reach the Spice Islands.

Magellan no longer wanted to sail around the tip of Africa. He wanted to sail west. Magellan was sure he could find a water passage through the Americas. He would then reach the Spice Islands from the east. There, Magellan would fill his ships with goods. He would then continue west until he reached Spain again.

King Charles liked Magellan's plan. He agreed to help him.

King Charles of Spain agreed to help Magellan.

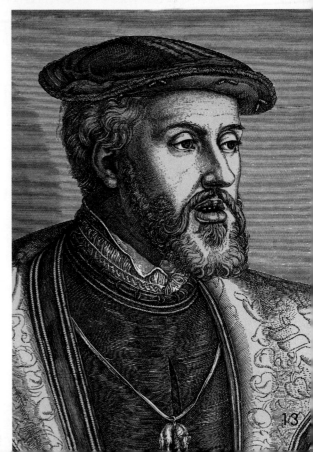

13

Chapter 4

The Voyage

On September 20, 1519, Magellan set sail from Seville, Spain. He had five ships and 277 men under his command. The ships were called the *San Antonio*, the *Trinidad*, the *Victoria,* the *Concepción*, and the *Santiago*. Magellan sailed aboard the *Trinidad*.

Trouble began early in the **voyage**. Some of the men started a **mutiny**. They did not want Magellan to lead them anymore. These men tried to take over the ships. But Magellan stopped them. He punished the men who led the mutiny.

Magellan led his five ships on the long voyage across the Atlantic Ocean.

Crossing the ocean was hard. Storms brought high winds. At other times, no wind blew. The ships needed wind to fill the sails and push them forward. While the ships floated, the Sun beat down on them. The heat rotted the food.

▲ Magellan used the stars to guide his ships. The position of the stars helped him know where he was.

South America

The ships finally reached the coast of South America in December. The men got fresh food and water. They also fixed the travel-worn ships. On Christmas Day, the ships headed south again. Magellan was sure a strait was near.

The ships sailed south for three months. They explored every bay. No passage was found. As they traveled farther south, the weather grew cold. Powerful waves damaged the ships. On March 31, 1520, Magellan led his ships into a **harbor** to rest.

In the Harbor

The next day, some of the men started another mutiny. They took control of three of the ships. But Magellan did not give up. He and his friends fought those men. Magellan got the ships back. Once again, he punished the men who led the mutiny.

In June, the sailors saw a man on the shore. He was almost naked. His face and body were painted different colors. The man danced and threw sand on his head. But Magellan and the sailors were more surprised at the man's size. He was more than 7 feet (2 meters) tall.

▲ Magellan called the tall man and his people Patagonians. This image shows a Patagonian man in 1780. Today, Patagonians are known as Tehuelches.

The sailors met more of the tall people. The tall people were friendly. But then Magellan tried to force two of them to return to Spain with him. The tall people fought Magellan and the sailors. Magellan decided it was time to move on.

FACT!

The *Santiago* was destroyed by a powerful storm in July 1520.

On the voyage, the sailors saw animals they had never seen before, including penguins. One group of South American penguins was later named after Magellan. These penguins ▼ are Magellanic penguins.

18

The Strait

In August 1520, Magellan ordered the ships to sail south. Once again, Magellan and his ships explored all of the bays. He was sure they would find a strait.

In October, the ships reached a deep, wide waterway running west. Magellan sent the *Concepción* and the *San Antonio* ahead to explore it. The ships returned two days later. They had found the strait.

▲ One of the men on the voyage drew this map of the strait.

Chapter 5

Victory

The ships sailed through the narrow strait for many weeks. Rocks and cold weather made the journey hard. Along the way, some sailors took the *San Antonio* and sailed back to Spain.

On November 28, 1520, the three remaining ships reached another ocean. The water was calm and smooth. Magellan named it the Pacific. In Spanish, *pacifico* means calm.

Islands

Magellan was sure the Spice Islands were very close. He only had to cross the ocean. But Magellan did not know that the Pacific Ocean was even bigger than the Atlantic Ocean.

This map shows ships sailing through the strait that Magellan found.

The trip across the Pacific Ocean was long and difficult. Magellan and his men ran out of food. To stay alive, they ate leather, sawdust, and rats. Many of the men became sick, and some died.

21

While crossing the Pacific, 19 of the men died from scurvy. They got this disease because they did not eat enough fruits and vegetables. Their skin turned yellow, their arms and legs swelled up, and their teeth rotted.

The ruler of the Philippine island of Cebu welcomed Magellan.

Finally, on March 7, 1521, the ships reached an island. Magellan and his men fought the people there and got fresh water and food. They then continued west.

A few days later, they reached more islands. These islands later were named the Philippines. The people there were friendly. They also agreed to serve the king of Spain. Some of the people became **Christians**.

Magellan learned about the nearby island of Mactan. The people there did not want to serve the king of Spain and become Christians. Magellan decided to make an example of them.

The End of Magellan

On April 27, Magellan and about 60 men went to Mactan. More than 1,500 people were there. They were ready to fight Magellan and his men.

The battle was short. The islanders shot poisoned arrows and spears at Magellan and his men. Magellan told his men to go back to the ships. On the way, the islanders killed Magellan.

Magellan was killed during a battle on the island of Mactan.

23

Chapter 6

Completing the Circle

Magellan's ships continued without him. Only 115 of his men were still alive. There were not enough men to sail all three ships. The men burned the *Concepción*.

In November 1521, the men found their way to the Spice Islands. They filled the *Trinidad* and the *Victoria* with spices. They then started the long trip around the tip of Africa to go back to Spain. Along the way, the *Trinidad* sank.

The *Victoria* returned to Seville on September 8, 1522. By then, only 18 men were still alive. They were the first people to sail around the world.

The *Victoria* was the first ship to sail around the world.

Lasting Impact

Ferdinand Magellan's voyage changed everyone's understanding of the world. Magellan showed that the world was much bigger than most people believed. He also showed that most of the world was made of water, not land. Most importantly, Magellan showed that the oceans were connected. It was possible to sail all the way around the world.

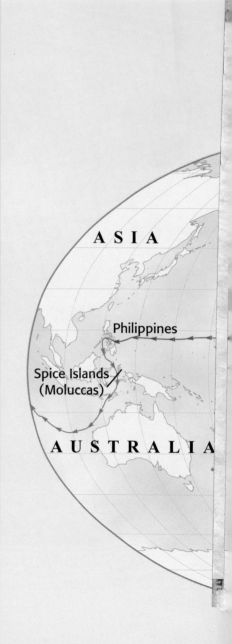

ASIA

Philippines

Spice Islands
(Moluccas)

AUSTRALIA

The Voyage around the World, 1519–1522

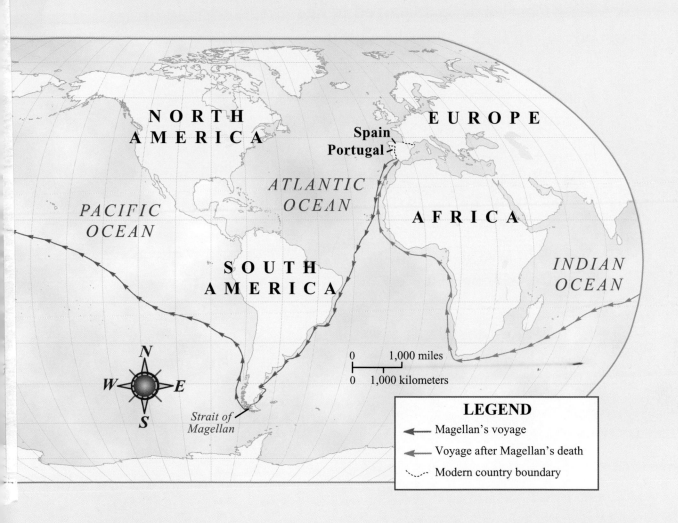

NORTH AMERICA

EUROPE

Spain
Portugal

ATLANTIC
OCEAN

AFRICA

PACIFIC
OCEAN

SOUTH
AMERICA

INDIAN
OCEAN

N
W E
S

Strait of
Magellan

0   1,000 miles
0   1,000 kilometers

LEGEND
← Magellan's voyage
← Voyage after Magellan's death
‥‥ Modern country boundary

Fast Facts

- Magellan grew up in Portugal. When he was a young man, he went to Africa, India, and southeastern Asia.

- King Charles of Spain agreed to help Magellan with his voyage to find a strait through the Americas.

- Magellan sailed down the east coast of South America until he found a strait to another ocean.

- The Spanish word *pacifico* means calm. Magellan named the ocean the Pacific because the water looked so calm.

- Magellan was killed on April 27, 1521, during a battle with the islanders of Mactan.

- Eighteen of Magellan's men made it back to Spain in September 1522. They were the first men to sail around the world.

Time Line

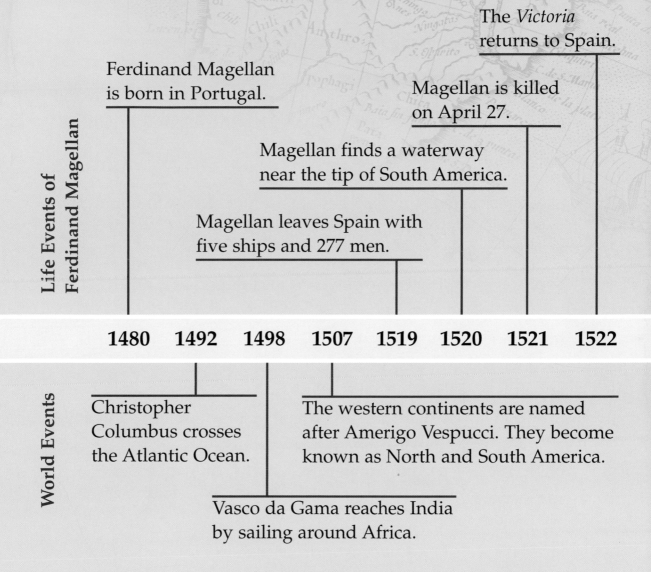

Life Events of Ferdinand Magellan

Ferdinand Magellan is born in Portugal.

The *Victoria* returns to Spain.

Magellan is killed on April 27.

Magellan finds a waterway near the tip of South America.

Magellan leaves Spain with five ships and 277 men.

| 1480 | 1492 | 1498 | 1507 | 1519 | 1520 | 1521 | 1522 |

World Events

Christopher Columbus crosses the Atlantic Ocean.

The western continents are named after Amerigo Vespucci. They become known as North and South America.

Vasco da Gama reaches India by sailing around Africa.

Glossary

bay (BAY)—a part of the ocean that is partly enclosed by land

Christians (KRISS-chuns)—people who believe in the religion of Christianity; Christianity is based on the life and teachings of Jesus Christ.

claim (KLAYM)—to say that something belongs to you or that you have a right to have it

explore (ek-SPLOR)—to travel to find out what a place is like

harbor (HAR-bur)—a place where ships shelter or unload their cargo

mutiny (MYOOT-uh-nee)—a revolt against someone in charge

page (PAYJ)—a young man in service to some member of a royal court or to a knight

strait (STRAYT)—a narrow strip of water that connects two larger bodies of water

voyage (VOI-ij)—a long journey

Internet Sites

FactHound offers a safe, fun way to find Internet sites related to this book. All of the sites on FactHound have been researched by our staff.

Here's how:
1. Visit *www.facthound.com*
2. Type in this special code **0736824871** for age-appropriate sites. Or enter a search word related to this book for a more general search.
3. Click on the **Fetch It** button.

FactHound will fetch the best sites for you!

Read More

Burgan, Michael. *Magellan: Ferdinand Magellan and the First Trip Around the World.* Exploring the World. Minneapolis: Compass Point Books, 2002.

Hurwicz, Claude. *Ferdinand Magellan.* Famous Explorers. New York: Powerkids Press, 2001.

Molzahn, Arlene Bourgeois. *Ferdinand Magellan: First Explorer Around the World.* Explorers! Berkeley Heights, N.J.: Enslow Publishers, 2003.

Index

Africa, 7, 8, 12, 13, 24
Asia, 7, 10, 11, 12
Atlantic Ocean, 5, 8, 15, 20

bay, 4, 16, 19

Charles, King (of Spain), 13
Christians, 22
claim, 6, 12
Columbus, Christopher, 8
Concepción, 14, 19, 24

da Gama, Vasco, 8

Europe, 8, 10, 11

harbor, 16, 17

India, 6, 7, 8, 10, 11

Mactan, 22, 23
Magalhães, Rui de, 6
Manuel, King (of Portugal), 12
Mesquita, Alda de, 6

Moluccas. See Spice Islands
mutiny, 14, 17

Pacific Ocean, 5, 20, 21
page, 6
Patagonians, 17
penguins, 18
Philippines, 22
Portugal, 6, 7, 11, 12

San Antonio, 14, 19, 20
Santiago, 14, 18
silk, 10
Spain, 11, 13, 14, 18, 20, 22, 24
Spice Islands, 10, 12, 13, 20, 24
spices, 10, 24
stars, 6, 16
strait, 4, 5, 16, 19, 20, 21

Tehuelches. See Patagonians
trade, 10, 11, 12
Trinidad, 14, 24

Victoria, 14, 24, 25